ALTRINCHAM
A Pictorial History

The railway line to Altrincham was opened in 1849 by the Manchester South Junction and Altrincham Railway (M.S.J. & A.R.) Company. This station was built in 1881 to replace the stations at Altrincham and Bowdon. The elaborate tower with its four-faced clock is still a feature of the scene today and its picture is often used to represent Altrincham. The cabbies' hut and the elaborate verandah have gone. By 1937 there were 130 trains between Manchester and Altrincham each day.

ALTRINCHAM
A Pictorial History

Hilda Bayliss

Phillimore

1996

Published by
PHILLIMORE & CO. LTD.
Shopwyke Manor Barn, Chichester, West Sussex

ISBN 1 86077 034 7

Printed and bound in Great Britain by
BIDDLES LTD.
Guildford, Surrey

List of Illustrations

Acknowledgements

I wish to express my gratitude to the following for permission to reproduce illustrations: Altrincham Grammar School for Boys Archives, F.W. Bamford, Mrs. E. Barnett, British Gas Archives, M. Brookes, Budenberg Gauge Company, K. Cooper (Record Electrical Company), M.A. Davies, Mrs. B. Fleming, I. Donaldson, Mrs. V. Harrop, R. & P. Higginbottom, Imperial War Museum, Lancashire and Cheshire Antiquarian Society, C.J.B. Lightfoot, M. Minifie, A. Morrison, G. Morton, J. Pendlebury, C. Perkins, Mrs. S. Percy, Police Museum Archives (Crewe), D. Rendell, Miss M. Ross, V. Shaw and G. Wright. Thanks are due to Hale Civic Society and Trafford Local Studies Centre for allowing access to their excellent collections and B.D. Morrison for the use of a drawing. I also wish to thank Mrs. J. Britton, Mrs. E. Denby, Mrs. V. Freeman, C. Hill, J. Pendlebury, D. Rendell, I. Sandham, G. Thornton and the staffs of Budenberg Gauge Co. and Record Electrical Co. for their patient help, also my husband without whose encouragement this book would still be a sheaf of papers in my desk.

Introduction

Altrincham lies eight miles south-west of Manchester, has a population of about 40,000 and is part of a mini-conurbation lying in the south-west part of Trafford Metropolitan Borough. It is an attractive dormitory town for Manchester and an important shopping and commercial centre. Before 1974, when the provisions of the Local Government Act (1972) made it an integral part of Trafford, it was a municipal borough in the county of Cheshire. It is surrounded by other residential places: Bowdon, Hale, Timperley and Dunham Massey, with which its buildings are contiguous, so that in some directions only the old township signs denote a change of district.

It is believed, from spot finds and aerial photographs, that the area may well turn out to be rich in prehistoric sites, and though some have been examined, many have not yet been confirmed. There have been individual finds indicating possible Roman and Romano-British sites, and an important Roman road passed near the town, along the line of the present A56 between Manchester and Chester. The name Altrincham was not recorded in Domesday Book of 1086 but a place seems to have been in existence from early Anglo-Saxon times, though perhaps not important enough to be individually recorded in the book. Evidence for its existence prior to the Norman Conquest is indeed slender, resting only on the interpretation of its name being Anglo-Saxon, according to J.Mc.N.Dodgson of the English Place-Name Society, meaning 'the place of Aldhere's people'. By the time of King Edward the Confessor it lay in a Saxon estate owned by a Saxon thegn named Alfward. The Normans, under William the Conqueror invaded north Cheshire from Yorkshire in a brutal campaign of 1070 called 'the harrying of the north'. Alfward's lands were seized and given to Hugh Lupus, the Norman Earl of Chester who then transferred them to one of his henchmen, Baron Hamon de Massey. Descendants of the first baron de Massey were to inhabit their caput at Dunham, two-and-a-quarter miles from Altrincham, for a quarter of a millennium until the sixth Hamon de Massey died in the mid-14th century. Today Dunham Massey is a stately home run by the National Trust, but in the Middle Ages there was a castle there, the home of the Masseys, replaced firstly by a hall in medieval times and by another in Elizabethan times.

The name Altrincham does not appear to be written in any document until 1290. The place probably remained a village until King Edward I issued a Royal Charter to the fifth Hamon de Massey of Dunham Massey allowing him to hold a market each Tuesday at Altrincham and a fair annually, on the eve, day and morrow of the feast of the Assumption of the Blessed Virgin Mary, 13-15 August. In the same year Hamon de Massey affixed his seal to a charter creating a borough at Altrincham, witnessed by Sir Reginald Grey, Humphrey de Beauchamp and Richard de Massey (knights) and others. The provisions of the charter encouraged burgesses to settle in what Beresford thinks was a 'planted' town laid out with a grid-iron of streets. As well as being given a burgage plot, two by five perches on which the burgess could build a house, grow vegetables, rear animals or devote to crafts, he was also given an acre strip in the open Town Field to the west of the town on which to grow corn. The measures in use were Cheshire measures where a perch was eight yards, not the statute five and a half yards. The two pieces of land could be sold, given, mortgaged or bequeathed by the burgess to another person but not to the king or a member of the church.

To the east along Timperley Brook and adjacent to a large bog called Hale Moss the burgesses had use of meadows. They could also use the common land and woodland to the north and east, and Hale Moss, for wood and grazing their cattle and pigs. The burgesses had many other privileges including free movement through the baron's lands, not having to work his lands and were able to attend fairs in all the de Massey lands without paying dues. Corn, however, had to be ground at the lord's mill, probably a water mill in the town, worked by a stream from Hale Moss, and 1/18th of the grist had to be given as multure. A toll was also levied on pigs at the feast of St James. The borough was a trading unit and an appropriate court called the Portmote was granted to administer law and government. Reeves, bailiffs and other officers, who regulated the safety and well-being of the inhabitants, were appointed from among the burgesses under the aegis of Hamon de Massey or his steward. Later a Court Leet and Court of Pie Powder developed out of the Portmote.

Certain activities carried out by the later Court Leet had probably also been carried out by the earlier court. Constables upheld law and order and brought to trial miscreants of minor criminal and civil actions that were settled locally by a jury appointed from among the burgesses. Major cases were tried at the Court of the Hundred of Bucklow, in which Altrincham lay, or the County Court at Chester. Other responsibilities were to protect the water supply, keep the borough free from undesirables and regulate the quantity and quality of food and drink, and guard against fire (the chimney looker was very important at a time when roofs were thatched). The dog muzzler was necessary to prevent bites and nuisance of dogs, some perhaps rabid. The ale taster's post was not as attractive as one might imagine at a time of unregulated brews. The Court of Pie Powder regulated the fairs and summarily dealt with offences. The first record of the appointment of a mayor dates from 1348 and this may mark the change from the Portmote to a Court Leet. There is an almost complete record of every Altrincham mayor from 1452 until 1974.

In 1319 another Royal Charter was issued confirming the first charter but changing the date of the fair to the eve, day and morrow of St James Day, 24-26 July (this became known as the Sanjam Fair). In about 1342 Hamon VI died without a legitimate heir, the de Massey dynasty ended and for 150 years Altrincham along with the rest of the de Massey estates passed by sale, marriage or death to various owners. A disastrous event was the Black Death of 1348-9 that must have taken its toll as elsewhere, for a manuscript of this date lists only 45 tenants in Altrincham holding 127 burgages.

Partly by inheritance and partly by purchase, the lands and farms of the de Massey estates (except for lands on the Wirral) were acquired by the Bothe (Booth) family from Barton north of the Mersey and in 1494 almost the whole estate was in the hands of William Booth. More lands were added over the years and in 1626 Warrington was obtained for the estate by donations unwillingly given to 'Old Sir George Booth' by his tenants, including the burgesses of Altrincham. Sir George started to replace the medieval hall at Dunham with one in the Elizabethan style. During the reconstruction, the last of the castle buildings were obliterated including the keep tower, which was probably sited on the circular mound by the side of the present hall. At the start of the Civil War Sir George was an old man favouring reconciliation between the contending factions but when this could not be achieved he and his grandson George supported the Parliamentarian cause. The younger man had a change of heart and was imprisoned in the Tower of London for supporting the restoration of the monarchy but was released without trial. After old Sir George had died and Charles II had regained the throne, the king gave George, the grandson, the title Lord Delamer for his support. In 1682 Lord Delamer and his son Henry entertained the Duke of Monmouth because they were disturbed by the fact that the king's brother James, the heir to the throne, had declared himself to be a Catholic. Henry was imprisoned in the Tower of London with Monmouth but was released without a trial. After the death of his father Henry became the second Lord Delamer and was again involved with Monmouth, leading to two further incarcerations in the Tower. On the first occasion he was released without trial, on the second he was tried for treason by Judge Jeffreys but acquitted. His experiences do not seem to have daunted him because in 1688 he led a troop of men, including some from Altrincham, to support William of Orange when he landed to claim the throne. For his part in this successful coup he was given the title Earl of Warrington.

During the 17th century dairy farming became more important in the area and in 1684 the lord of the manor, Henry Booth, the second Lord Delamer, had a butter-market built in the market place at Altrincham. It was a six-sided building with a court room above the open market room and a lock-up, known as 'the dungeon', to house wrong-doers. In the turret hung a bell with the inscription 'Delamer 1684 Donum pr. Nobile Henry Domine', which had been cast at Little Budworth, a village 10 miles to the south-west. In the market place there were also some stocks, a whipping post and a cross. The first two structures were used as alternative punishments to incarceration in the dungeon or being fined. An example of a fine or amercement of the period in a court roll of 26 April 1699 states, 'The Town Fields [should] be enclosed on 2nd February each year and that person that neglects making up his payments [for the use of the fields] by that time appointed shall be amerced in ten shillings [50p]'.

The political adventures of the various members of the Booth family during the latter part of the 17th century had cost a great deal of money and when Henry died in 1694 his son George inherited a run down estate with many debts. George decided to devote his efforts to rescuing the fortunes of the family by careful personal administration of the estate. The rentals of 1704, reveal that 62 tenants of the Altrincham part of the estate had to provide the following: 11 capons, 14 hens, four loads of coal to the manor, 24 loads of turf and a further 84 loads of turf were to be got ready for carting. Services such as ploughing, reaping, mucking out and guttering were also to be undertaken. In times of war nine tenants were expected to give 'general' service to the lord and others supplied 14 halberts and eight muskets. Almost all the Altrincham land was arable, very fertile and at an average value of £1 12s. 3d. per acre, was the highest rated of the estate lands in Cheshire. In 1702 George married the heiress of a rich London merchant and used her dowry to continue to refurbish the Elizabethan mansion of Dunham Hall, to improve Dunham Park and to increase the holdings of the estate. Through his efforts, on his death in 1758 his only child, Mary, became a very rich heiress. She had married Harry Grey, the 4th Earl of Stamford, in 1756 and they divided their time between their estates at Dunham, Bradgate in Leicestershire and Enville in Staffordshire.

The extension of the Bridgewater Canal to Dunham had been one of George's wishes but it was not until 1765, seven years after his death, that the canal was constructed along the 83 ft. contour, providing transport for people and goods between Worsley, Manchester and eventually Runcorn. The *Packet House* and *Navigation Inn* at Broadheath provided shelter and refreshment for passengers and there were warehouses for storage of goods. Agricultural produce and textiles, stone, timber and coal were transported and Altrincham became a more prosperous place. Nightsoil from Manchester was used to fertilise the farmland round the town, which became an important centre for vegetable production.

As well as marketing agricultural produce from the fields and market gardens, many inhabitants of Altrincham were involved in the textile trade of spinning combed worsted wool in their cottages. According to Aiken in 1795, the wool to be spun was brought to Altrincham market by Manchester merchants and the finished products were then taken away. During the 18th century the population increased considerably and in Georgian times a period of house rebuilding occurred in Higher Town (Old Market Place and Market Street), partly for rich incomers wanting to live in the ambience of an exclusive, elevated, small market town which was within commuting distance of Manchester. In the early 19th century, Altrincham was only lightly affected by the Industrial Revolution. Two or three mills were built in the Woodside area for cotton spinning—competition from Ireland having ruined the worsted trade—and one for corn. The workers lived mainly in cottages in Lower Town, the George Street area. This factory industry declined and by 1841 only 72 people were listed in the textile trade: bobbin makers and people who spun in their cottages; The one remaining mill ground corn. The most surprising statistic is that the most numerous occupation in the town at that date was that of servant.

The main roads were improved by turnpike trusts. After the canal was built in 1765, the trustees of the turnpike from Manchester, which ran parallel to it, immediately improved the road to counter the loss of trade to the canal. Stage coach companies operated services between Manchester, Chester and places in north Cheshire, using Altrincham as a stopping place. Old Market Place was the transport and commercial focus and here the chief inns, the *Red Lion, Waggon and Horses, Roebuck, Unicorn* and *Stamford Arms*, were all stopping places and the last two were also staging posts where a change of horses could be obtained or a coach and horses hired. In *The Confessions of an English Opium Eater*, De Quincy described the bustle and colours of Altrincham market place that he could see below his hostelry window.

Although a railway system had been established in Manchester 19 years earlier, the lines for the Manchester and South Junction Railway with its terminus at Altrincham were not laid until 1849. The first train to arrive was greeted with celebrations and people were encouraged to migrate to the town. Lord Stamford built a new town and market hall adjacent to the *Unicorn* in 1849, perhaps a reflection of the prosperity he expected would follow the arrival of the railway. Rich cotton merchants, now able to live away from their factories, yet travel easily to them, built mansions on the higher ground to the west and south-west of the town. Victorian terraces were built round the core of the town and to the east, some replacing older property that had become very dilapidated. Cottages for workers were built in Chapel Street and New Street on land not governed by the strict building laws which Lord Stamford applied to the houses built on his land. Many people with little money lived in lodging houses. The character of the town changed and some affluent people who had moved to Altrincham earlier in order to live in an exclusive area moved out to Bowdon and Hale because they felt that the town had lost this ambience.

For centuries, Altrincham's spiritual needs were catered for by the parish church at Bowdon, less than a mile away, all christenings, marriages and funerals taking place there. Chapels-of-ease were built at Ringway and Carrington, but being without resident incumbents, they were vulnerable to seizure. Ringway Chapel was taken over by Dissenters who were themselves evicted when a member of the Crewe family (of Crewe Hall), who was not kindly inclined to their beliefs, inherited the area which included the chapel. The Dissenters built a chapel at Hale in 1723 and adopted Unitarianism about 1750. The first chapel in Altrincham was built by the Wesleyan Methodists in Chapel Walk (now Regent Road) in 1788 but it was not until the last year of the 18th century that Anglican St George's was built as a chapel-of-ease to Bowdon (becoming a parish church in 1868). The first incumbent of St George's was Oswald Leicester. Many other fine places of worship were built during the 19th century: the New Connexion Methodist Chapel in George Street in 1821; St Margaret's Dunham Road in 1855; the Roman Catholic church, St Vincent de Paul in 1860. The Wesleyan Methodists built Bank Street chapel in 1866, and their original building in Chapel Walk (Regent Road) was taken over by the members of the Congregational faith. Dunham Road Unitarian Chapel opened in 1872 and the Altrincham Baptist Church was built on Hale Road in 1878. The Primitive Methodists built a chapel in Oxford Road in 1878 and the Wesleyan Methodists built St Paul's Chapel in Enville Road in 1880; it was later demolished. Although the Welsh Presbyterian Chapel was planned at this time it was not opened until 1903. Eventually the various branches of Methodism combined to build a new church on Woodlands Road in 1968.

Altrincham began the 19th century with a population of 1,692 and this grew tenfold over the century. This rapid increase caused problems in law and administration and it became apparent that the Court Leet, though aided by the Town's Meeting of influential persons and members of the Vestry, could not effectively administer the town. The Cheshire magistrates appointed a High Constable for the hundred of Bucklow, in which Altrincham lay, in 1829 but the Court Leet continued to police the town until 1857 when the Cheshire Constabulary replaced the court's constables. The fire service run by the Court Leet had little equipment and no full-time officers. For some time the head of police took over the fire service. Eventually the Urban District Council of 1894 built a fire station and appointed a brigade.

There was much illness in the town and a government inspection was sought in 1848. Following the inspector's report a Local Board of Health was set up in 1851 to improve the roads, create a drainage system and administer the town. A drainage scheme was adopted and a works built at Sinderland, north of the town, to which sewage was diverted from Timperley Brook. Altrincham Smallpox and Cholera Hospital was built on Hale Moss in 1840 by the township authorities, but it soon proved too small for the large number of cases arising from the town's insanitary living conditions. A larger hospital nearer the town replaced it in 1850, built as a memorial to E.J. Lloyd (magistrate, of Oldfield Hall) by his wife and named after him, the land having been given by Lord Stamford. It treated cases of infection and of accident occurring to poor and destitute persons of Altrincham and Bowdon. A patient with a broken leg could find himself in the next bed to a patient suffering from cholera. The Local Board took over the running of Lloyd's, and when it proved inadequate, built the Altrincham Provident and Dispensary Hospital in Market Street in 1870. The two hospitals served the community until 1911 when Lloyd's was closed and an Isolation Hospital was built in Sinderland Road, which later became a maternity hospital but is now closed. Altrincham General, the former A.P.and D., still serves the community as an out-patient clinic and elderly people's rehabilitation centre, but this too is due for closure.

After the creation of the Local Board in 1851 the Court Leet became largely ceremonial. Its last administrative function was the supervision of the market, but this ceased in 1878 when the Local Board obtained the right to hold a market from Lord Stamford and opened a Market Hall at the corner of Shaw's Lane and Market Street in 1879. Altrincham acquired an Urban District Council in 1894 and a new town hall in Market Street in 1900. The leader of the council was a chairman, the post of mayor being reserved for the elected head of the Court Leet, and the two posts existed side by side until the formation of the Municipal Borough in 1937.

Education was not available for Altrincham children until 1759 when a school was founded at Oldfield House, with money left by Thomas Walton, a salt master. There were places for 40 boys from Hale, Bowdon, Altrincham and Dunham. In 1867 new premises were built at Seamon's Moss that were used until the school closed in 1938. In 1783 Oswald Leicester started a Sunday school for children, one of the first in Cheshire, on Ashley Road. The school was moved to larger premises, the Poplars in Norman's Place, provided by Mr. Leicester's father, an Altrincham grocer. After Oswald had been inducted as the first vicar of St George's, he continued his work with children and was instrumental in the building of the Jubilee School in 1810. In time, all the Anglican and Roman Catholic churches and the Non-Conformist chapels provided Sunday and week-day schools to instil religious beliefs and to teach children to read, write and calculate. The schools also served to keep children off the streets when laws were passed regulating the employment of children. There were several private and dame schools but these were not subject to inspection and were mainly short-lived.

In the 19th century central government began to accept its responsibility to educate the younger generation and made grants to the church and chapel schools. Later these grants were only paid when attendance and standards of competence in reading, writing and arithmetic were accepted by the government's examiners. Attendance at school became obligatory up to the age of 10 in 1880, 11 in 1893 and 12 in 1899 but in spite of these regulations many children were kept off school to assist in the home or to work in the fields. A School Attendance Committee was formed in 1891 in Altrincham to provide free elementary education and to ensure regular attendance and, by 1898, it was providing 3,169 places for elementary pupils. Irregular attenders were tracked down by School Board Officers, a job previously undertaken by the teachers in their spare time. Cheshire County Council was made responsible for education in the area in 1903 and a sub-committee was appointed in Altrincham to manage elementary education. Elementary schools were built at Navigation Road and Queens Road (now Stamford Park), and in 1910 a school for higher elementary education was opened in Queens Road. The County High School for Girls (Altrincham Grammar School for Girls) and County High School for Boys (Altrincham Grammar School for boys) were built in 1910 and 1912 respectively. The schools were fee-paying but it was possible to obtain a free place by passing an examination. Attractive schools were built for children living on the new estates at Oldfield Brow, and Timperley and old buildings were also replaced. A wider curriculum was adopted to enhance the children's knowledge, physical fitness was encouraged and visits were arranged to broaden their horizons.

Georgian and Victorian house building proved inadequate during the 20th century when the population continued to grow not only by natural increase but by 'in-migration'. The addition of parts of Dunham Massey and Carrington, following the Altrincham Extension Act of 1920, increased the population census figure to 25,513. The addition of Timperley and urban parts of Dunham Massey in 1936 created a total of 36,133 persons. Figures for subsequent censuses show continued slow growth to 41,122 in 1961. After two decades of slight decline the 1991 figures showed that the population was stabilising at about 40,000. The increasing population needed extra houses and shops. In Broadheath the Linotype and Machinery Company, which opened in 1897, built a model village for its workers and provided leisure activities and playing fields for them. Altrincham Urban District Council built a council estate in the Urban Road area in 1905. Further development was halted by the outbreak of the First World War but was continued after 1918. During the 1920s and '30s many private houses were built. Families from older properties were re-housed in council estates built on Oldfield Brow. After the Second World War some pre-fabricated houses were built with a life expectancy of 10 years; they are still inhabited. Clearance of the Chapel Street and New Street cottages necessitated wholesale demolition and a rebuilding programme of flats and small houses took place. Many of the inhabitants were moved to the Broomwood council estate at Timperley. Some of the large villas of the district were subdivided to provide flats, or demolished to provide sites for blocks of flats or town houses with a higher density occupancy. Although horse transport and trains were an established part of the scene extra transport was needed for a more mobile population and a tram service to Manchester was introduced in 1907 by Manchester Corporation. Although a few privately owned buses were operating in the area before the First World War, services were extended afterwards to Macclesfield, Stockport, Latchford, Lower Peover, Oldfield and Northwich. Journeys to holiday places were available for a public not yet car-owning. Buses were introduced by Manchester Corporation replacing the trams in June 1931.

Part of Hale Moss was presented to the town in 1880 by Lord Stamford for the creation of Stamford Park. Cricket and hockey pitches, a municipal golf course and a football ground were created out of another part of the moss. In the town as a whole, people found a welter of sporting, artistic, theatrical and educational amenities available to them as baths, bowling greens, tennis courts, theatres, cinemas, a library and art gallery were provided. The nearby river Bollin was a popular place to swim and picnic. Parades to honour visits by royalty or to celebrate regal events attracted huge crowds. Educational services offered vocational and leisure training. Many societies were formed to encourage people's talents in singing, acting, instrument playing, painting, service to the community, and organising the town's trade and commerce.

From the end of the 19th century, part of Broadheath, formerly concerned with the canal trade, proved an ideal site for the development of heavy industry. Machine tools were manufactured by the George Richards Company. Tilghmans developed sand-blasting and joined Richards. The family firm of H.W. Kearns was another famous machine tool company that eventually also joined Richards. The Churchill

Machine Tool Company specialised in precision grinding machinery. Measuring instruments were produced by the Schaffer-Budenberg Gauge Company and J.W. Record Electrical Company. The Linotype and Machinery Company built printing machinery. Luke and Spencer made grinding machines and emery wheels and C.S.Madan were bronze founders. Thornton and Pickard invented and produced photographic equipment. In its heyday Broadheath employed more than 10,000 personnel. Altrincham became an industrial town with an international reputation for its products.

During the First World War Altrincham supported the country's war effort and many men volunteered. Those who did not return are remembered by a memorial designed by G.F. Armitage. A Roll of Honour was also mounted in Chapel Street which was described by King George V as 'the Bravest Little Street—in England'.

During the Second World War the area was subject to bombing and loss of life, but the firms in Broadheath continued to supply necessary tools, equipment and armaments; planes were repaired at Royles car-body repairing shop in Oakfield Road and shells were filled in the very centre of the town in a building in Market Street. To acknowledge the part Altrincham had played in the war King George VI and Queen Elizabeth paid a visit at the end of hostilities to Broadheath. The Broadheath area started to decline in the 1960s and now supports new retail shopping warehouses and small industrial units in purpose-built or adapted premises. However, some famous names such as Record, Linotype and Budenberg still survive in parts of their original buildings.

Altrincham cannot lay claim to many nationally known people. Victoria Crosses were awarded to Captain E.K. Bradbury in the First World War and Private W. Speakman in the Korean war. Helen Allingham, who spent the first years of her life in Altrincham, became the first woman member of the Royal Water-Colour Society. George Faulkner Armitage achieved fame for his designs for furnishing interiors of houses and clubs, and for his carvings. Ronald Gow was a writer of plays for the stage, the cinema and television. However, many unsung inhabitants benefited the town, businessmen who brought prosperity and those who performed voluntary work. Their names on the list of mayors in many cases offer proof of their commitment to the well-being of Altrincham.

In 1937 Altrincham was created a Municipal Borough by charter and the first mayor elected was Roger, 10th Earl of Stamford, the contemporary and last incumbent at Dunham Hall. Before his death in 1976, knowing that Altrincham had ceased to be independent and had become part of Trafford Metropolitan Borough, he requested that the Court Leet should be reformed to enact old customs to remind people of Altrincham of its history. It was revived in 1977 and still continues in a ceremonial capacity.

Today Altrincham is a busy market, commercial and residential town. It is linked by rail and bus to Manchester and north Cheshire and by a fast tram service to Manchester and Bury. It is amazing to think that next Tuesday a market will be held at Altrincham as it has been for over 700 years.

1 Burdett's map of 1777 shows that Altrincham (then spelt Altringham) lay in the north-east of Cheshire. Today it is part of the Metropolitan Borough of Trafford. The Manchester to Chester road closely followed the straight line of a Roman road. At an unknown date its line was diverted at Broadheath in the north to pass through Altrincham and rejoin the Roman road at the top of the hill south-west of the town near Highgate. The river Mersey was the northern boundary of Cheshire until 1974. Dunham Hall and Park, once the home of the lords of Altrincham, is now a National Trust property.

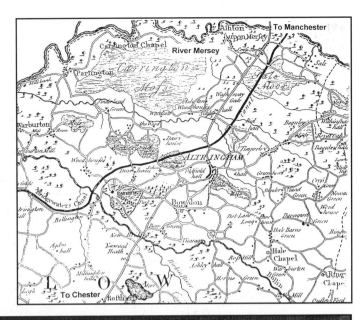

2 With this charter of 1290 Hamon de Massey, the fifth lord of Dunham, created a market borough at Altrincham, one of his many manors. He offered a plot of land in the borough and an acre of land in the open field to the new town dwellers, the burgesses, and laid down rules by which they would live.

3 This wax seal of the Massey lord was attached to the tape with which the charter was tied. The charter was not signed but witnessed by Sir Reginald de Grey, then justice of Chester, Humphrey de Beaumont and Richard de Massey, knights, and local lords such as Gilbert de Aston, Thomas de Acton, Hugh de Baguley, Matthew de Hale, Henry de Dunham and John de Bowdon.

4 A view of Dunham Massey Hall in 1697 by Knyff, engraved by J. Kip. The castle belonging to Hamon de Massey, Lord of Altrincham, had disappeared by this time but the keep had probably been sited on the mound to the left of the hall. The Massey dynasty lasted nearly three hundred years and was followed by that of the Booth family, one of whose members built the hall in Elizabethan times.

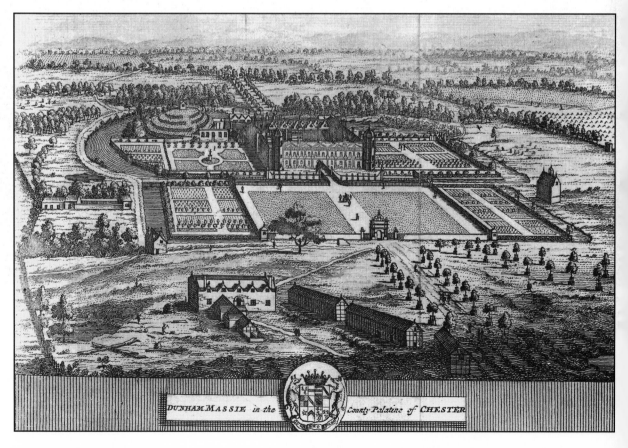

DUNHAM MASSIE in the County Palatine of CHESTER

5　The mid-17th-century mill in the grounds of the hall has an overshot wheel powered by water from the former moat. It was originally a corn mill but was altered in Victorian times to operate a saw. Its powerful machinery has been reconditioned and it is still known as 'The Dunham Ripper'.

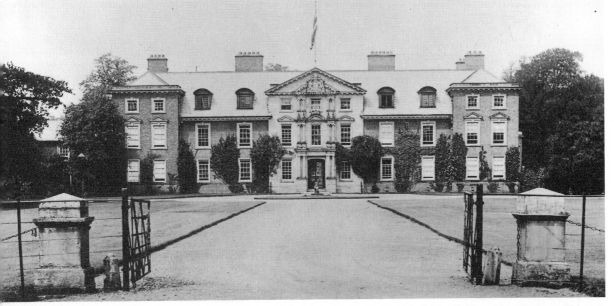

6 *Above left.* In the mid-18th century, the Booths were followed by the Earls of Stamford, some of whom did not live at Dunham. This picture shows the carriage of the 9th Earl and his Countess leaving Altrincham station in June 1906 when they returned to live at Dunham. The two men in the left foreground carry the staves of the Court Leet of the borough.

7 *Above.* The house was in a state of disrepair after being unused for many years and this picture shows Dunham Massey Hall after the 9th Earl had effected extensive repairs.

8 *Below.* A turn-of-the-century view of the earlier centre of the town, the old market place. The cab-stand was near the site of the former market cross. The picture was taken by a Panoram Camera developed in 1896 a wide-angle machine capable of covering 142 degrees.

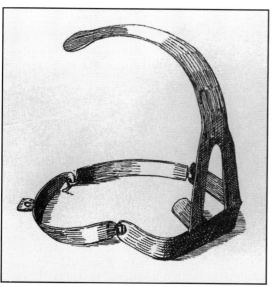

9 *Top.* The Court Leet for centuries was in charge of law and order in the town. The iron brank weighing 800g. was a crudely constructed instrument of punishment. The iron gag was placed in the mouth and the device was forced on the heads of nagging scolds, usually women, who were led round the town wearing it for all to see. It was reputedly used at the beginning of the 19th century when an accused woman refused to walk and was pushed round the town in a wheelbarrow.

10 *Middle.* Measures were used by Market Lookers appointed by the Court Leet to ensure that correct quantities were traded. These five brass containers hold 40, 20, 10, five and two-and-a-half fluid ounces. Markets were strictly regulated—no selling was allowed before or after the allotted times. Fines were imposed or punishment ordered, such as immersion by cucking (ducking) stool, for irregularities or poor quality products.

11 *Bottom.* This stone was erected *c.*1840 at the foot of the road called Higher Downs to show the boundary of the borough of Altrincham with Dunham Massey, a neighbouring township. Each year it is used as the starting point when the members of the Court Leet (now ceremonially) retrace the eight miles of the borough boundary.

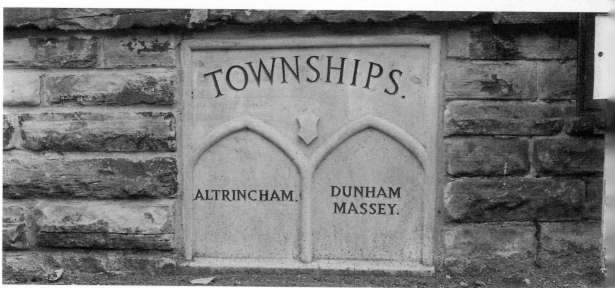

12 A peaceful view of the Bridgewater Canal looking towards Dunham from Broadheath, showing some of the chimneys of that industrial area. The stretch of canal from Worsley to Manchester and Lymm (via Altrincham) was built in 1765 and completed to Runcorn in 1776. Although there were only six furlongs one chain (1342 yards) of canal in Altrincham it had a great impact on the area, providing cheaper, quicker transport than by coach or packhorse.

13 Wharves, coal staithes (in the foreground) and warehouses (beyond) were built on the canal-side at Broadheath. From the late 19th century manufacturing firms such as machine-tool makers, gauge-makers, sand-blasters and printers built premises near the canal, using it to transport raw materials and completed artefacts.

14 The *Old Packet House* at Broadheath (canal behind) was the second stopping place on the journey from Manchester to Runcorn providing shelter for passengers and storage facilities for packages for despatch or collection. The 8 a.m. boat from Manchester stopped here at 10 a.m. on its way to Runcorn, which it reached at 5 p.m. and one arrived at 4 p.m. on its way to Manchester.

15 Although Altrincham had three mills at the beginning of the 19th century and was important for textiles and corn, little evidence of this fact remains. Mill House stood at the junction of Grosvenor Road and Derby Street. It was the home of the master of one of the nearby mills.

16 The road from Stockport to Altrincham was turnpiked in 1821. The Toll Bar at Timperley stood opposite the *Hare and Hounds Hotel*. Every vehicle, person or animal that passed the house could be seen from the angled windows and had to pay a toll, a lucrative source of income to repair and maintain the road.

17 The first Town and Market Hall was built by Lord Stamford in 1849, adjacent to the *Unicorn*, to replace the Butter Market and courtroom which stood in the Market Place. The clock tower was a copy of the one on the former building and the bell from there was incorporated into the tower and continued to be used to alert the townspeople of danger or to attract attention for important announcements. The Court Leet held its meetings here and the magistrates held Petty Sessions every Tuesday fortnight.

18 St Mary's Church, Bowdon, was an ancient foundation mentioned in Domesday Book. It was the centre of a huge parish and, with a dominant position 223 ft. above sea-level, can be seen from miles around. It was Altrincham's parish church until 1868. This was how it looked before the mid-19th century.

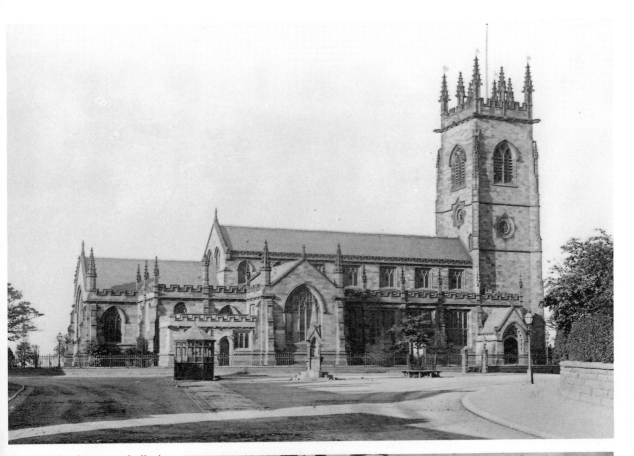

19 St Mary's was rebuilt in 1100, 1320, 1510 and 1858. This shows the church after the last rebuilding was carried out by the architect, William Hayward Brakspear. It contains medieval effigies, a fine 17th-century tomb and other monuments.

20 Ringway Chapel was one of two early chapels-of-ease in the large parish of Bowdon. During the Civil War the chapel was taken over by Dissenters who were themselves forced to leave by a member of the Crewe family, who had inherited land in the area, but who was not sympathetic to their cause. The chapel is now closed and the cross from there has been placed to the left of the entrance to St Mary's churchyard.

21 Hale Unitarian Chapel was built by members of the Presbyterian faith when they were evicted from the Ringway Chapel. From 1750 the congregation adopted Unitarianism. In 1906 a stained glass window was dedicated to Mary Worthington of Sale. It was designed by Burne-Jones and William Morris and is one of only three examples of their work in the area.

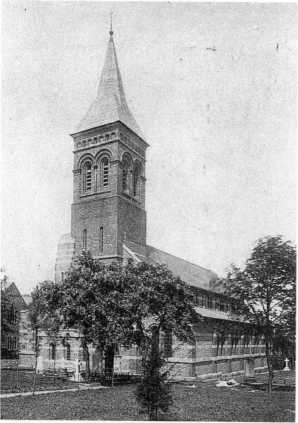

22 St George's was built near Old Market Place in 1799 as a chapel-of-ease to Bowdon parish church. When it was opened part of the Manchester road on which it stood became known as Church Street. A separate parish for St George's was created in 1868. The church remains continually open for prayer at the wish of the vicar and congregation.

23 This large Wesleyan chapel in Bowdon was built for Bowdon residents and partly to replace an earlier chapel on Regent Road. Its foundation stone was laid in 1874 but it was not consecrated until 1880 because of structural problems. Known as The Dome, it was described as 'the most ambitious building in Bowdon'.

24 An interior view of The Dome, also known locally as 'the sinking church'. Its copper dome turned green over the years and it was a landmark until it was demolished in 1965.

25 The red-brick Church of St Vincent de Paul, Bentinck Road, lies in the Roman Catholic diocese of Shrewsbury. Services were held in a house until the first Catholic church was opened in 1860. It was replaced by the present building which was opened on Rosary Sunday in 1905. While this church was being built services were sometimes held in a tent.

26 St John's Church, built in Early English style, was opened in 1866 to serve the rapidly growing number of people in Lower Town. The Newtown area of the parish near the railway became so populous that a daughter church, St Elizabeth's, was built in Pownall Street in 1890.

27 St Margaret's Church, in striking Gothic style, was built by the Earl of Stamford and consecrated in 1855. Although it stands only half a mile from Old Market Place, it lay in the township of Dunham Massey. Many Altrincham people attend its services. The spire which brought the church to a height of 210 ft. was considered unsafe in view of the heavy traffic passing along the A56 and was demolished in 1927.

28 The Unitarian Chapel was opened in 1872 to replace a meeting-room in Shaw's Lane. It was designed by Thomas Worthington and opened by William Gaskell, whose wife Elizabeth was the famous novelist.

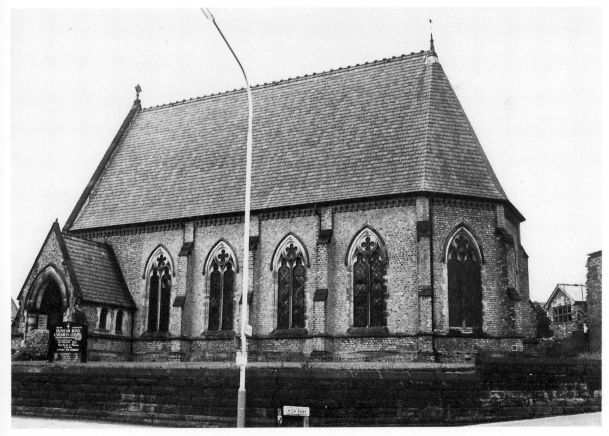

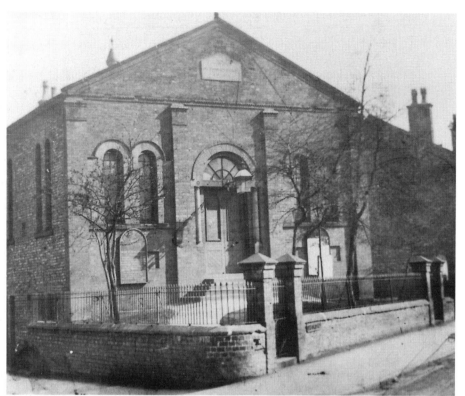

29 Hale Primitive Methodist Chapel was built in 1878 in Oxford Road for members of the faith who wanted to regain the earlier mores of Methodism and hold their services in a simple building. The Sunday school met in the basement until new premises were built in 1921 adjacent to the chapel. Since 1966 the building has been used by the Club Theatre.

30 Members of the Salvation Army are photographed holding a meeting on ground adjacent to the market hall which was later glassed over. Their headquarters were premises in Shaw's Lane, previously used as a meeting-room for the members of the Unitarian faith.

31 The lintels over the door of the police lock-ups in George Street built in 1838. High Constables for the Bucklow Hundred were appointed by the Cheshire Magistrates from 1829-56 to work in conjunction with constables of the Court Leet. A constable and his family lived here at the time of the 1841 census and the occupants of its three cells included an ironstone miner, a puddler, two labourers (one Irish), an 18-year-old painter and a chair-bottomer. The station was used until new premises were built in Dunham Road in 1866. After the lock-ups were demolished in 1974, the lintels were stored and later incorporated into a seat in Old Market Place in 1990.

32 Altrincham police force in 1904, shown here, numbered one officer and 21 men. During the First World War the depleted force was supplemented with special constables. By 1920 the force had increased to 65 officers and men. The men are wearing helmets (reserved for special duties and church parades) but continued until the 1930s to wear 'shako' hats for normal duties.

33 Altrincham fire brigade in 1920 consisted of one chief officer, one (full-time) engineer and 14 others operating from premises at the rear of the Town Hall. The area they protected included Altrincham, Bowdon and Hale U.D.Cs., Dunham Massey, Timperley, Ashley and Ringway. From 1919 it had been extended to include the whole of Bucklow Rural District, Sale and Ashton-upon-Mersey U.D.C.S. and Knutsford.

34 The Board of Health's offices in High Street (Market Street) from 1863. The Board was formed in 1851 on the recommendation of Sir Robert Rawlinson after his report that the health of the townspeople would be improved if a local government board was appointed to provide better sewerage and road surfaces and improve the water supply. The Board functioned until the formation of the Altrincham Urban District Council in 1894.

35 Altrincham General Hospital was called the Altrincham Provident Dispensary and Hospital when it was built in 1870. The hospital started with 44 beds when first opened but accommodation increased to 100 by 1937. In 1912 the average length of stay was 36 days but this was reduced by improved treatment to seven days in 1986. During the two World Wars beds were reserved for wounded servicemen.

36 Old and young shared wards as this picture shows. Staff uniforms were very formal as was the routine, though a small relaxation seems to have been made—a bird in a cage can just be made out. Not all operations took place here as an excerpt from the Navigation School Log Book shows: 'Fifth October 1909 Miss Buckley absent to wait on brother who is undergoing a surgical operation at home'.

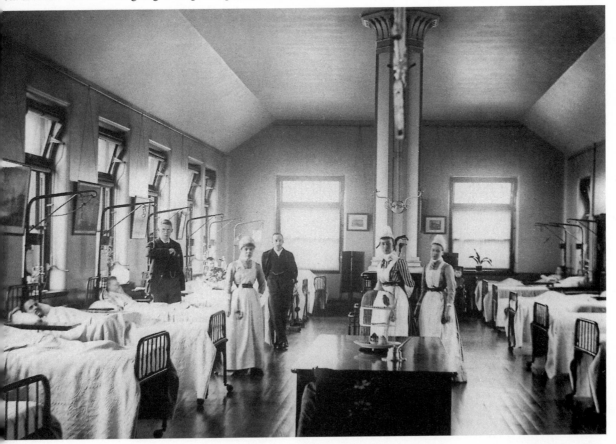

37 *Above left*. This petrol-driven ambulance replaced a horse-drawn vehicle in 1916. The service was not free. From 1930, however, journeys of less than 10 miles were provided free to residents of the area of the Urban District.

38 *Below left*. Altrincham Town Hall of 1900 was built in Jacobean style to the design of the architects Messrs. Davenport and Hindle for the Urban District Council. It replaced the 1849 building adjacent to the *Unicorn*. It ceased to be used as a town hall after the reorganisation of 1974 when Trafford Metropolitan Borough was created with a town hall at Stretford, six miles away, but it is still used as offices for some local government departments.

39 *Above*. The Council Chamber is an impressive room. The heavy oak furniture includes a seven foot high mayoral chair made from oak grown at Dunham Hall. Some of the windows contain stained glass depicting the shields of past dignitaries. A county court is held here three days a week.

40 *Below*. In 1759 a school was built at Oldfield House using money left by Thomas Walton, salt master, of Dunham Woodhouses, for the instruction of 40 boys aged eight to 11 years who lived in Altrincham, Dunham, Bowdon and Hale.

41 In 1867 new school premises were built at Seamon's Moss. The inscription states: 'This school was founded by Thomas Walton, gent. AD 1759. This building was erected AD 1867'. Many eminent citizens have been pupils at the school which was held in high esteem.

42 A class at Seamon's Moss in the 1920s. Although it was a school for boys, one girl was allowed to be a pupil, being the daughter of the headmaster at the time. The masters instructed the pupils in subjects normally taught in a grammar school. The school closed in 1938.

43 The tablet commemorates the founding of the first Sunday school in Altrincham in the upper storey of Tadman's Cottage on Ashley Road, Altrincham. Over one hundred children were reported to have attended the non-conformist school which was started by Oswald Leicester.

THIS TABLET
COMMEMORATES THE OPENING
ON THIS SITE
OF THE FIRST SUNDAY SCHOOL
IN ALTRINCHAM A.D. 1783
BY
OSWALD LEICESTER
AFTERWARDS THE FIRST INCUMBENT
OF S¹ GEORGE'S CHURCH
ALTRINCHAM

44 This house in Dale Street was procured in 1858 by members of the Primitive Methodists to be used as a Sunday school replacing one in the Newtown area. The buildings in the area in which it stood have been completely demolished.

45 The Jubilee School was founded by Rev. Oswald Leicester in 1810 on the occasion of the 50th Jubilee of the accession of King George III. The building stood south-west of the church and was in use until 1860 when a school was built nearer the church.

46 The Literary Institute was built in George Street in 1852 by the Altrincham and Bowdon Literary Society, to replace premises in Well Lane in which the society had been founded five years earlier. The building contained a reading room, three classroms and a library. In 1866 an extension was built to add a lecture hall. The whole complex was demolished in the 1970s.

47 This picture of a dormitory at Loreto Convent, *c*.1920, shows the use of curtains to ensure privacy. No modern conveniences here. The school had been founded in 1909 but was so successful that Bellefield on Dunham Road was purchased in 1913. Greenhouses, a coach-house and hay loft were all converted to classrooms until nearby property was purchased to provide extra teaching space.

48 Girls of St George's School practise a display of dancing to be performed at the celebration for the coronation of King George V and Queen Mary in 1911.

49 Girls of St George's School make a pretty picture holding garlands of flowers used in one of their dances.

50 St Margaret's Primary School was built in the Albert Street/Chapel Street area, Altrincham, although the church stood in Dunham Massey township. An excerpt from the School Log Book reads: 'August 29th 1863. The school feast took place last Wednesday, the day was moderately fine. The children all went to Knutsford and had their treat on the race-course, the children travelled in vans. There was a slight accident on reaching Knutsford, some of the children fell out of the van through a form falling out but there were none injured. It was quite dark when we returned home and some of the children were fast asleep'.

51 Aerial view of Altrincham Grammar School for Boys which was founded in 1912 by Cheshire County Council and named the County High School. The school became known as Altrincham Grammar School from 1934 even though it was situated in Bowdon.

52 The County High School cricket team of 1915 includes Ronald Gow front right, Mr. Jedson stands to the left of the team and Mr. Laver, the headmaster, to the right. Mr. Gow later returned to the school to become a much respected teacher.

53 *Left.* A physics class in the County High School in 1924. The writing on the blackboard suggests that a lesson on 'Light' is in progress.

54 *Below left.* Craft lesson in the County High School in 1924. The scene of industry marks it as an interesting and well-liked lesson.

55 *Below.* Altrincham Grammar School sports in 1947. J. Adair, who was a very good athlete, was photographed making a long jump which set a record.

56 Children of Stamford Park School play-acting in the 1920s. The school, for pupils from non-conformist schools in the Altrincham area, was built by a sub-committee formed by Cheshire County Council It was opened in 1906 and had separate entrances for infants, girls and boys.

57 *Left*. The rocking-horse named Dobbin was very popular at Stamford Park Infant School. The horse was used only for birthdays when the lucky child rode the horse with a friend in each of the two baskets. Mrs. V. Harrop, seen here as a child, is sitting second from the right on the second row in this photograph of *c*.1936.

58 *Below left*. A class of girls in the 1930s proudly hold examples of their handiwork at Stamford Park School. Mrs. Fleming, as a child, is sitting second from the right on the first row. She remembers making and embroidering the hessian pyjama-cases under the guidance of Miss Hartington, a very popular teacher.

59 *Below*. Class photographs were taken in 1935 at Stamford Park School to commemorate the silver jubilee of King George V when each child was also presented with a pewter mug. The celebration continued with games and refreshments on Bradbury school playing fields.

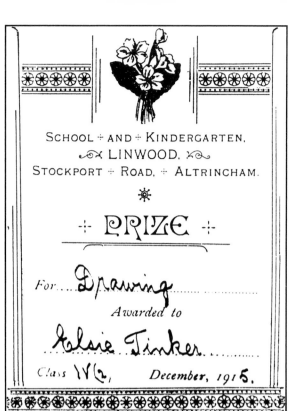

SCHOOL + AND + KINDERGARTEN,
~~ LINWOOD, ~~
STOCKPORT + ROAD, + ALTRINCHAM.

✲

+ PRIZE +

For *Drawing*

Awarded to

Elsie Tinker

Class IV (2,   *December,* 1915.

60   *Left.* Bookplate of a prize presented at a private school December 1915. There were many private schools in the area, most of which proved ephemeral.

61   *Right.* Houses on the Oldfield estate. The estate was built as a response to the growing population after the First World War. The land on which the Urban District Council built this large estate had been parts of Dunham Massey and Carrington which were added to Altrincham in 1920.

62   *Below.* Fir Tree Farm, Timperley, was built by Humphrey Paulden in 1676 on the edge of Timperley Common. The farm was demolished in 1934 and the site is now occupied by a supermarket and part of Timperley village. Timperley was added to Altrincham in 1936.

63 The *Pelican Hotel*, West Timperley, lies along the path of the Roman road from Manchester to Chester and some coins of that period were found when the hotel was being altered. The original inn was built in Elizabethan times. There was a healing-well nearby and visiting invalids stayed at the inn. It is said to be haunted by the ghost of Thomas Brennan, known as Timperley Tom, who was hanged on Bucklow Hill for the murder of Jacob Pott of Hale on 30 December 1790. A reward of £100 was offered for his capture. The following rhyme was written on a poster after the hanging, 'Good people now be warned by me, If I had never done this deed, I would not hang upon this tree, But be alive in Timperley'.

64 The *Pelican* after rebuilding. No Sunday licences were available but it was possible to get a drink if one had travelled more than three miles. The inn did a great business serving drinks to cyclists from Stretford and Manchester.

5 Old Hall, Timperley was a farm built by James Wood early in the 19th century. Nearby, surrounded by a moat, is the site of the medieval hall which was occupied until 1847. It was only after the medieval hall was completely demolished that this building became known as the Old Hall. It is now a hotel.

6 This 16th-century cottage stood at the market place end of Well Lane (Victoria Street). This cottage and the buildings on this side of the lane were demolished in 1932 for road widening. Part of the way down the lane, one of the town's wells was discovered. It was excavated by the South Trafford Archaeology Group a few years ago and found to be a circular brick construction 16 ft. deep standing on a square wooden sill. It had been in use until 1880. Over two thousand pieces of pottery were found dating from the 14th to the late 19th centuries. Only a few metres away a tippler toilet was discovered! Conjunction of drinking water and sewage waste created major health problems in Altrincham, acerbated by the rapidly growing population during the Victorian period.

67 Richmond House, Norman's Place was typical of many Georgian houses built on the south-western outskirts of the town for wealthy people who moved to the area from the dirt and grime of Manchester.

68 Stamford Estates Office and National Trust shop. This late 18th-century building has a pilastered doorway and a fine elliptical staircase. The earl's steward Hugo Worthington lived here.

69 A group of late Georgian houses in Norman's Place drawn by Mr. B.D. Morrison.

70 Culcheth Hall, a mansion built in Victorian times, was once occupied by Ellis Lever, a wealthy coal merchant. In 1891 Miss Edith Lang and her father founded a girl's school here which has recently celebrated its centenary.

71 Townfield House was a Victorian mansion occupied in 1852 by William Armitage, a cotton manufacturer. During the First World War the house was purchased, equipped and furnished by Mr. John Leigh (later Sir) and was lent to the Red Cross Society to be used as a convalescent home for injured officers. It was known as the John Leigh Hospital.

72 Holmeside in St Margaret's Road, was a Victorian mansion built for Mr.W. Melland, a cotton master who lived in the pleasant air of Altrincham but who had his factory amidst the smoke and grime of Stockport.

73 Cottages in George Street, which was a narrow cobbled lane in Victorian times. Gradually the street changed its function from residential to retail and public buildings.

74 Houses were built in the Moss Lane area at the beginning of this century. Many are privately owned and have been tastefully refurbished.

75 These cottages in Denmark Street, built in Victorian times for workers, have recently been demolished for road widening.

76 Some of the houses built by the Linotype printing machinery firm for its workers at Broadheath. The estate of rustic cottage-type properties was built in the style of a garden suburb with trees and broad roads. There were different styles of houses for different grades of workers.

Altrincham, Ce

77 General view of George Street after the cottages and farms had been replaced by shops at the beginning of the century. It was the middle of the day and the blinds were used to protect the articles in the windows from fading. The hems of the long skirts of the ladies were lined with tape to reduce wear and soiling as they walked along the pavement.

78 *Below*. A view of George Street in the 1930s. Both cars and horses were modes of transport but the former were beginning to outnumber the latter. The street was still lit by gas lamps even though the Electric Supply Company had offered in 1897 to light the 430 street lamps for £140 less than the U.D.C. was then paying for gas.

79 *Right*. These fine buildings on Stamford New Road were designed by J. MacNamara for J.H. Broun, whose initials appear among the intricate terracotta mouldings along with the shield and motto of the Urban District Council. Attractive gas lights illuminated the shop windows.

80 *Below right*. A general view of The Downs in 1905. The message on the back of this postcard begins, 'Ordered a coat today - £2'. Though sold as a postcard the picture is in fact back to front.

81 Shops on Church Street show how busy the retail area near Old Market Place was for many years even after the market was moved in 1879. All the property on the left has been demolished for road widening. The first building on the right with a large lamp is now a fish and chip shop.

82 Standing in front of the butcher's shop at 12 Ashley Road are Bill Lathom, Bob Gatley and Les Pendlebury. Mr. Gatley was the owner of the shop and the first President of the Altrincham Chamber of Trade and Commerce. It was usual to display meat outside one's shop in the early part of the century.

83 Pendlebury's shop at 22 Lloyd Street was decorated to celebrate the coronation of King George V on 22 June 1911. From left to right are Miss Devaney, John Dykeman (cab-driver wearing a bowler hat), Leslie Pendlebury and Leslie Hewitt. The girl on the step in a white blouse is Miss May Pendlebury. The man holding the child is the owner William Henry Pendlebury and his eldest daughter Miss Ida Pendlebury peeps over his shoulder.

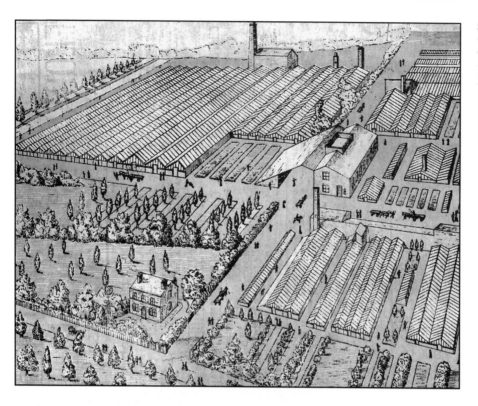

84 A view of part of the Oldfield Nurseries, Altrincham, owned by W. Clibran and Sons. The fine sandy soil of the Altrincham and Timperley area was very fertile and eminently suitable for growing market garden produce and for nurseries.

85 & 86 Attractive cover of *Clibran's Seed Catalogue* for 1895. The business notice, *below right*, shows what a large organisation it was, owning land in North Wales as well as locally.

Nº 131

DESCRIPTIVE CATALOGUE 1895
OF
VEGETABLE AND FLOWER SEEDS

SEED TRIAL GROUNDS
URMSTON, NEAR MANCHESTER.

Wᴹ CLIBRAN & SON

SEED MERCHANTS,
10 & 12 MARKET STREET, MANCHESTER

OLDFIELD NURSERIES AL

& PRINCIPALITY
LLANDUDNO JUNCTION.

WM. CLIBRAN & SON'S
CATALOGUE OF SEEDS, &c., FOR 1895.

BUSINESS NOTICES.

EARLY ORDERS.—As the Seed Season is necessarily a short one, we shall feel obliged by our Customers sending in their orders as soon as possible after receiving our Catalogue.

ORDER SHEET.—It will expedite the despatch of orders if our patrons will make use of the accompanying order sheet, and particular attention is requested to have the name and address inserted, to prevent disappointment and delay.

CATALOGUES.—We often have complaints of Catalogues going astray in transit, and we esteem it a favour if customers will inform us when they do not receive them at the usual periods, so that another copy may be sent. When customers change their residence we shall be pleased if they will furnish us with their new address.

FREE CARRIAGE.—All Seeds are delivered free, excepting orders under 5/-, containing Peas, Beans, Potatoes, &c.

TERMS OF PAYMENT.—Accounts due Quarterly and Half-yearly strictly net: 5 per cent. discount allowed of Seeds and Bulbs, and 2½ per cent. off Plants, Trees, &c., for cash with order or on receipt of Goods. Cut flowers, Wreaths, Bouquets, &c., are all sold for prompt cash and no discount. *Postal and P.O. Orders to be made payable at Altrincham.* Small amounts may be remitted in Penny Stamps, but no receipt will be sent for sums of 2/6 and under, unless Stamp is enclosed to cover postage.

NOTICE TO OCCASIONAL CUSTOMERS.—To keep a mass of petty accounts for small orders causes great inconvenience and loss: we must therefore request prepayment of them. No customer should feel offended on this ground, as it is not a question of giving credit, but of book-keeping. In making remittances be careful to send sufficient to cover the amount of goods ordered. In cases of short remittances, we will limit the order to the amount of money received. We are compelled to adopt this rule on account of the inconvenience and expense of collecting small balances.

RETURNED PACKAGES.—Boxes, Baskets, &c., which have been forwarded with Seeds, will be allowed full price for when returned. *The name and address of sender must be on the address label. A Post Card should also be sent us advising of their despatch.*

HOME GROWN SEEDS.—Some firms profess that all the Seeds they sell are grown at home; sensible people will, however, doubt the veracity of such statements: but we do say that all the Seeds we sell are PURE and RELIABLE, and selected with the greatest possible care, no effort being spared to have the best of everything, and we thoroughly test the germinating powers of all seeds before they are sent out. Our strains of Primula, Cineraria, Calceolaria, &c., have a wide reputation, and Seeds of these are carefully selected in our nurseries from picked plants.

EXPORT ORDERS.—Seeds, Bulbs, &c., specially selected for exportation to all parts, and carefully and securely packed in air-tight cases. Plants packed in Wardian cases, &c.

NOVELTIES.—We are always open to purchase plants or seeds, upon proof of quality, of anything new and choice, and shall be pleased to hear from patrons possessing them.

✦ NEW SEED AND BULB WAREHOUSE.

To meet the rapid development of every department of our business we are compelled each year to increase the extent of our grounds, warehouse and storage accommodation, and number of employees. This is very gratifying to ourselves, as it is an unquestionable proof of the success of our endeavour to please our customers, and our best thanks are due to those patrons who have so kindly interested themselves on our behalf in recommending us to their friends, and thereby helping to build up our present large trade.

In 1892 we had the pleasure to announce the opening of our Rose Nursery, at Llandudno Junction, owing to the increasing demands for our Roses. Again in 1893 we were compelled to seek fresh quarters for our Seed Trial Grounds on account of the limited room at our home nurseries, and a suitable place was taken at Urmston, near Manchester.

In addition to our Shops in Market Street, Manchester, we have had large rooms for Storage, &c., but for some time the accommodation has been inadequate, and we have now secured a large and commodious warehouse, which has been fitted up with every convenience for dealing with an immense volume of trade. The new premises will be entirely devoted to the order trade in Garden Seeds and Bulbs, and special provision has also been made for dealing with the increasing demand for our Agricultural Seeds.

ESTABLISHMENTS.

The telephones at our establishments are connected with the National Telephone Company's System, thus enabling customers in London, Liverpool, Birmingham, Leeds, and most large towns, to hold direct communication with us, and have their urgent orders placed in hand at once.

Bulb and Seed Stores, 10, Market St., **MANCHESTER.**
Farm Seed Warehouse, 10, Cromford Court, **MANCHESTER.**

Telephone No. 170.

Cut Flowers, Bouquets, Wreaths, &c., 12, Market St., **MANCHESTER.**

Telegrams : "CLIBRAN, MANCHESTER."

Plants, Trees, &c., Smithfield Market, **MANCHESTER.**
The Oldfield Nurseries, ALTRINCHAM, } CHESHIRE.
The Stamford Nurseries, BOWDON,

Telephone No. 14.
Telegrams : "CLIBRAN, ALTRINCHAM."

The Principality Nurseries, LLANDUDNO JUNCTION, NORTH WALES.
Seed Trial Grounds, URMSTON, near MANCHESTER.

7 This is Whittle's Farm which stood near Seamon's Moss School. Mr. Whittle, on the left, drove round Altrincham in a horse and cart selling vegetables produced on the farm. Mr. Spence, on the right, is entering the building from which produce was also sold.

8 Crickmore's saddlery and harness shop. Saddlery was an important business when most of the transport was by horses. When a husband sold his wife (as happened in Old Market Place c.1823) he had to provide a halter to put over her neck for her to be led away by her purchaser. This would only be a small part of the saddlery trade!

89 Chemists were very important sources of advice as well as medicines in Victorian and Edwardian times, when visits to the doctor were expensive luxuries for poor people. This branch of Tootill stood at the foot of the Downs within easy reach of Lower Town and the densely populated Newtown area. Note the gas lamps in the doorways of these shops.

0 Minifie's was a very successful grocery and confectionery shop on Hale Road which opened in 1909, closing in 1922 when the essor needed the premises or other purposes. The akes, pies and potted meats old in the shop were made t the Minifies' home in Vestgate, Hale and transorted in baskets by Mr. Vaterhouse, Mrs. Minifie's ather. Their products were o popular that very often he first bake was sold en oute to the shop and urther batches had to be prepared.

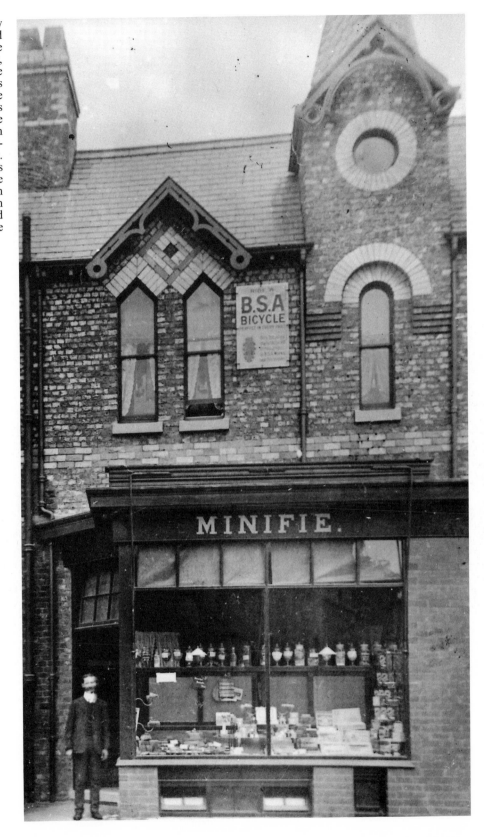

91 This posed picture of a family at the turn of the century was taken by Mr. W. Peters, owner of the Crown Studio. The Noble family was very musical and two of the gentlemen are shown playing instruments, a guitar and a mandoline, the belly of which was made of striped veneers. The boys are in sailor suits, popular dress for small boys.

92 The Noble family moved from premises in Church Street to the shop in Railway Street to sell musical instruments. They moved premises later to 53-55 George Street (now occupied by a building society) where they also sold furniture. The firm gave a 10-year guarantee with every piano sold.

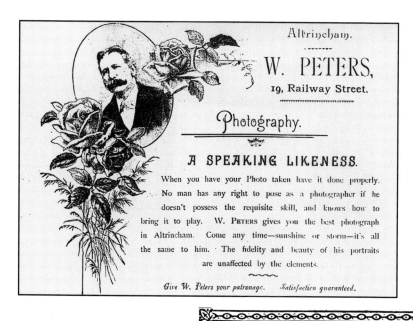

Altrincham.

W. PETERS,
19, Railway Street.

Photography.

A SPEAKING LIKENESS.

When you have your Photo taken have it done properly. No man has any right to pose as a photographer if he doesn't possess the requisite skill, and knows how to bring it to play. W. PETERS gives you the best photograph in Altrincham. Come any time—sunshine or storm—it's all the same to him. The fidelity and beauty of his portraits are unaffected by the elements.

Give W. Peters your patronage. Satisfaction guaranteed.

93 Many professional photographers offered their services at a time when very few people owned their own cameras. An advertisement for Mr. Peters whose premises at 19 Railway Street still has the large upper window which provided extra light for his studio.

❋ BAZAAR DECORATIONS. ❋

THE NOVELTY ART Co.,

3, STATION ROAD, ✛ ALTRINCHAM,

BAZAAR FITTERS AND DECORATORS,

Are prepared to undertake, in whole or in part, any work connected with the supply of materials, and fitting of halls and rooms for Bazaars or Entertainments. A special feature is made of Floral Designs, which produce Artistic Effects not easily otherwise obtained. Being ourselves the manufacturers of this Floral Material, it is supplied direct from our own workshops for each Bazaar, and is therefore always fresh and new.

SCENERY AND DRAPERY SUPPLIED AND FITTED.

We also Supply ON HIRE, Curtains, Screens, Entertainment Fit-Ups, &c.

ENTERTAINMENTS PROVIDED ON HIRE OR SHARING TERMS.

Illusions, Side Shows, Shooting Galleries, Aunt Sally, Cocoa-Nuts, Waxworks, Tableaux, Conjurers, The Phonograph, The Kinetoscope, and the latest money taker, The CINEMATOGRAPHE.

Agents for the latest Fun Producing Novelty. **CONFETTI** Sold in bags or supplied on Sharing Terms.

FAST SUPERSEDING RICE FOR WEDDINGS.

NOVELTY ART CO., 3, STATION ROAD, ALTRINCHAM.

94 This advertisement shows the range of items obtainable from The Novelty Art Co. Confetti is noted as taking the place of rice at weddings and the 'cinematographe' was the 'latest 'money taker'.

✈ G. B. BRADSHAW & CO., ✈
Portrait Painters and Photographers.

LATEST SPECIALITY:

Large Portrait in handsome gold frame and cased complete, with half-dozen Cabinet Photographs, only 21s.

Why can we finish Paintings and large Portraits cheaper than any other Firm? Because we are Artists, and finish for many of the Principal Photographers in the Kingdom.

Cabinet Photographs from 12s. 6d. per doz.   Cartes-de-visite from 5s. per doz.
Our Speciality, 3 Cabinets, 6 Cartes, for 6s. 6d.   Musical Photograph Albums, from 21s.   Views of Bowdon, Alderley, Knutsford, &c.

SHOW ROOMS AND STUDIO OPEN FROM 9 to 9.

HIGH BANK, CHURCH STREET, ALTRINCHAM.

95 This advertisement for G.B. Bradshaw shows the long hours traders stayed open in Victorian times. His prices must have been very competitive.

96 Mr. E. Cryer, Purveyor of Grocery, photographed outside his shop at 23 Stamford Street. Tomatoes at 7d. per pound, boiled ham at 8d. per quarter pound, eggs at 2s. 2d. for 12, butter at 1s. 3d. per pound give some idea of the cost of food in the 1930s.

97 *Above.* The *Unicorn* had a dominant position at one end of the market place and was probably the most important inn in Altrincham. The present building dates from the early 19th century but records refer to events there in the 18th century. The first meeting to consider extending the Bridgewater Canal to this area took place there. It was a posting station, auction room, excise office and on this occasion was used as hustings for Coningsby Ralph Disraeli when he contested the seat in the General Election of 1895.

98 *Above right.* The *George and Dragon* and *Wheatsheaf* lie at the north end of Church Street, the north entrance to Altrincham town in olden times. Before this stretch of road was called Church Street, the *Wheatsheaf*'s address was Turnpike Road. Stage coaches stopped at the *George and Dragon* on their way between Manchester, Knutsford and Northwich.

99 *Right.* The *Orange Tree* in Old Market Place was named after a public house on Railway Street which had burned down in 1855. The front of this inn conceals a medieval timber-framed building. The next building to the left was a french-polisher's, then came the *Horse and Jockey*, a beer-seller and next door was the *Red Lion*, a popular place for lodgings for troops and travellers.

100 In 1841 there were 20 inns, public houses and beer-sellers in Altrincham. By 1860 the population had doubled as had the number of places selling alcohol. The *Royal Oak*, Victoria Street was one of these being first licensed to sell ale and porter in 1852. There was another public house of the same name in Stamford Street.

101 The bank was designed by George Truefitt in Cheshire 'magpie' style for W.C. Brooks in 1877 when he moved his banking business from 40 Church Street. The main banking hall with 32 ft. high stained glass windows was flanked by a house on each side, one for the manager and one for the assistant manager. Mouldings of Mr. Brooks's initials and shield on the building were retained when the bank was taken over by Lloyds. The patterned, tiled roofs and the chimneys are particularly attractive.

102 Mr. J. Pendlebury and Mr. A.B. Brookes (later to found an undertaking business) among a group of cabbies photographed outside their hut whilst waiting for fares. The cabbies provided a useful service for travellers who did not have their own conveyances at a time before there were regular bus services.

103 A coach of the old stock of the M.S.J. & A.R. is being pulled by an L.M.S. 2-6-2 Fowler tank engine. After 1931 the line was electrified providing a cleaner, cheaper and more frequent service, but steam trains had to be used from Altrincham towards Chester. Overhead wires can be seen here. Re-electrification in 1971 was partly paid for by the sale of the copper overhead wires used in the earlier system. The lines are now used by the Metrolink tram system linking Altrincham with Manchester and Bury.

104 Some coaches were lit by oil lamps but others were lit by gas. The compartment in the picture holds a folded leather bellows-type bag which was refilled from small gas-producing plants at Altrincham and other railway stations. The compartments were located next to the guard's van and each set of bellows would be able to provide illumination for four coaches.

105 Horse-bus laden with passengers ready to start its journey. The names Altrincham and Delamere can be seen on the destination board. Many horse-buses around Altrincham and in north Cheshire acted as collecting services for the railway passengers; others tapped areas where the trains did not go.

106 Horse-buses in Altrincham en route from Knutsford to Manchester. They are seen in George Street, which is unusual as the coaches normally travelled via the Old Market Place.

107 Many people rode their own horses and many of the bigger houses had their own stables. A pony and trap in Goose Green, *c.*1915.

108 Some people had their own traps. This trap is probably similar to one in which Mr. Cryer, the grocer who lived in Stamford Street, took his daughter to Stamford Park School.

109 This picture shows Broadheath bridge, one of the original crossings of the Bridgewater Canal, being altered when Manchester Corporation extended its tram system to Altrincham in 1907. The trams could not cope with the hump-backed bridge so it was lowered; it was also widened at the same time. A small tipper on a rail track is moving earth to the canal for transport away while a steam digger works on the other side. The *Navigation Hotel* can be seen behind the digger.

110 The first tram-car, a four-wheel balcony car number 263, at the tram terminus on an inspection run 30 April 1907. The service started nine days later when six decorated trams were cheered into the town. The service continued until 1931.

111 A tram from Piccadilly passing a parade in Stamford New Road. The 47s (to Manchester Piccadilly) and the 48s (to Deansgate) provided cheap transport for several decades from Altrincham. From 5 November 1923 the 47 service had a mobile mail-box on its 8.26 p.m. tram, where letters could be posted if the evening collection had been missed.

112 *Above.* Open-top tram No.493 at the terminus outside the *Downs Hotel* which in 1864 had been a posting house with a licence to let horses. Early in this century there was a cab-rank outside and on one occasion it is reported that some members of the Band of Hope serenaded the cabbies with a rendering of 'My drink is water-bright from the crystal stream' whereon the cabbies signed the pledge to become teetotal—much to the concern of the landlord. Fortunately for him their teetotalism only lasted a week.

113 *Above right.* This passing-loop along Sandiway enabled one tram to travel into Altrincham while another simultaneously travelled to Manchester on nearby Barrington Road. Timetabling was most important to allow trams to travel in opposite directions on the same stretch of the loop at the same time. In the distance is a tram going into Altrincham. Manchester Corporation introduced buses on the Manchester to Altrincham route to replace the trams from 1931, a passing loop was not necessary and Sandiway again became a quiet road.

114 *Right.* The solid-tyred lorry stands outside the premises of John Wood at the corner of Ashfield Road and Moss Lane. The furniture removal firm also ran coach trips and a few buses on local services prior to the First World War. After 1918 the firm under Fred Wood extended the bus services to Stockport, Northwich, Lower Peover, Macclesfield as well as locally. From 1926 the North Western Roadcar Company (N.W.R.C.) took over Wood's vehicles and routes.

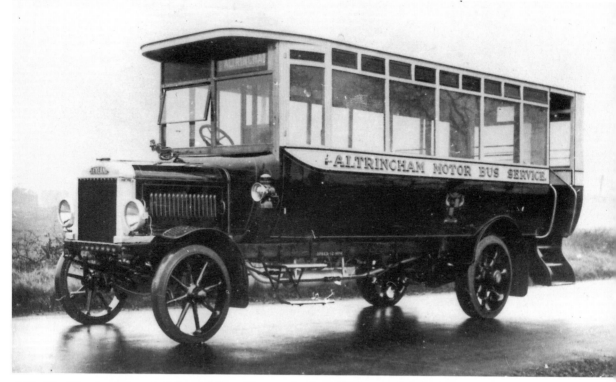

115 The Wood company had four of these 32-seater Leyland G7 buses which had a maximum speed of 12 miles per hour. In 1922 when the chairman of the company, Mr. A.R. Ireland, was the mayor of the Court Leet, and the director of the company was the chairman of the Urban District Council, the firm had Altrincham's coat of arms painted on the side of their vehicles. This is just discernible.

116 In Kingsway is a 40-seater bus No.MB 7751 built by Leyland. It is one of Wood's fleet which was taken over by N.W.R.C.; their logo has been painted over the Altrincham coat of arms.

117 Mr. A.B. Brookes stands at the side of a Jaguar, one of the first wedding cars in Altrincham. He also drove private ambulances and started an undertaking business (*see also* no. 102).

118 A horse-driven hearse comes out of Brewery Street on to Cross Street on its way to a funeral. The undertaker Mr. Brookes had premises at 42 Stamford New Road where his wife served teas in a room above the funeral parlour. Being buried with ham off the bone was considered an essential send off.

119 *Above.* A peaceful scene on Hale Moss, which was a natural wilderness before it was developed for industry, leisure complexes and housing.

120 *Above right.* The Earl of Stamford presented 16 acres of Hale Moss to create a recreation area for the people of Altrincham. The layout was designed by Mr. John Shaw F.R.H.S. and Stamford Park was opened in 1880. The bandstand was a popular source of entertainment, concerts were held here regularly and, on one occasion in 1899, two thousand people were reported to have attended to hear the Altrincham Borough Band.

121 *Below.* The bowling green in Stamford Park. Bowling had long been a favourite sport in Altrincham and one of the first greens in the county had been situated at the *Stamford Arms & Bowling Green Hotel*, now the site of the Cresta Court.

122 Mr. Benjamin Clegg was the first secretary to be appointed to the Altrincham and Bowdon Literary Institute building when it was transferred to the Local Board of Health in 1877 and became a Free Library for the inhabitants. A rate of ½d. was adopted to fund it.

123 These cottages in George Street were demolished so that the Free Library could be enlarged in 1892.

124 The enlarged Free Library premises included a Technical School. Engineers from Broadheath industries, using their skill and knowledge, often helped with lessons for apprentices. The school continued until 1923 when the classes were moved to the Navigation Road Evening School.

125 *Above*. The river Bollin early this century. Within walking distance of Altrincham, the Bollin valley was a popular place to relax and picnic. It was also an attractive place to swim.

126 *Below*. The Bollin shown in a different mood in 1925 when thousands gathered to witness a baptismal service conducted by Rev. Cowell Lloyd, minister of Altrincham Baptist Church.

127 *Above right*. Swimming was a popular activity and it was decided in 1897 to build the Jubilee swimming bath to commemorate the Diamond Jubilee of the accession of Queen Victoria, hence the name. The committee pose for a picture to record the opening of the bath in 1900.

128 *Below right*. Altrincham had a water polo team, shown here *c*.1912. A second bath had been added in 1909 and swimming was added to the curriculum at many schools. A board recording the names of successful swimmers in 1909 has recently been found and refurbished at Stamford Park School.

129 *Above left.* Altrincham's first scout group was formed in 1909 by Mr. I. Plant for boys of St Alban's Church, Broadheath. The troop was registered on 27 January 1911 as 1st Broadheath and the British Red Cross Society presented them with colours. It was a very active troop training the boys in moral duties as well as the delights of camping.

130 *Above.* The picture shows the opening parade of Altrincham Show, *c.*1910. The first show was held in 1861 when one of the main occupations of the area was agriculture. The aims of the society were to encourage agriculture and promote the breeding of stock. From 1896 Devisdale became its permanent home where, apart from the war years, it was held annually until 1966. Some of the animals were brought by train and the Downs was closed to traffic so that they could walk to the ground. A bus service from Altrincham ran pedestrians to the show but the cost of sixpence was considered very overpriced.

131 *Left.* Horses were a very important part of life for use on the farm as well as for leisure and transport. The horses on show here were competing for one of the prizes at the Altrincham Show. Although the 1895 show had only made £37 profit, 27 more classes were added for 1896 and the prize-money was increased to £1,250, enlarging what was already claimed to be the biggest one-day show in Britain.

132 Cycling became an alternative form of transport to horse-riding at the end of the 19th century. This party from Altrincham halt at Great Budworth. Riding three-wheeled cycles are, left to right: Miss Royle, Miss Hampson, Mr. W. Walker, Mrs. MacNamara and Mr. A. Cowsell.

133 Enthusiasts, including members of the Hughes family, dentists in Altrincham, take a break on one of their outings. The ladies prefer the stability of three-wheeled machines but some of the gentlemen daringly ride bicycles which needed long legs to attain any speed and avoid falling off.

134 *Above*. The banner understood to be at an Altrincham Fair advertises the Great American Bioscope, which firs appeared in America in 1894 and was introduced here *c*.1896. The bioscope was produced by the Warwick Tradin Company and was one of the most popular projectors. The films listed were *La Defense du Drapes* (Defence of th Colours) and *Les Dernières Cartouches* (The Last Cartridges). They were 53 ft. long and would only run for on minute each.

135 *Above right*. The size of membership of the Altrincham Gardeners' Society indicates the interest and importanc of this pastime. Before the advent of the numerous garden centres, people exchanged cuttings and seeds grown in thei own gardens and this society would provide a useful place for such transactions.

136 *Right*. As well as providing housing for its employees the Linotype Company encouraged leisure activities. Thi group of performers was called the Linettes.

MUSIC HALL

137 Visits by royalty were times for celebration. This arch was one of two built by James Hamilton (at a cost of £140) to welcome the Prince and Princess of Wales on the occasion of their visit on 4 May 1887. This arch spanned Dunham Lane from Groby Road to the Unitarian Chapel, the other spanned Station Road (Kingsway). During the 15-minute visit local schoolchildren sang two songs for their Highnesses in Old Market Place. After the visit the children, led by the battalion band of the Cheshire Royal Volunteers, walked to the Green Walk entrance of Dunham Park for refreshments and games.

138 Sanger's Circus, 1895, on its way to Hale Moss for its annual visit, which was one of the town's highlights, as an entry in the Log Book of St George's school shows: '27. 6. 1897 Attendance this afternoon poor, possibly owing to a circus being in town'.

139 Parades were always well attended. This one *c.*1900 passes the *Malt Shovels* and Springfield House (with the steps) and Springbank (later the site of the Hippodrome) on its way from Stamford New Road to George Street. Springbank was the home of Mr. J. Siddeley whose brewery at nearby Hale produced a beer nicknamed Siddeley's Purge. Its effects can be imagined. A record of a sojourn in the stocks was blamed on 'the surfeit of Siddeley's Purge'.

40 *Above left.* Newtown Prize Jazz Band was a very successful group which collected money for the hospital charity fund. It won many prizes and trophies for its performances and news of the results of competitions held away from the area was sent by homing pigeons to relatives and friends eagerly waiting in Altrincham. The photograph taken *c.*1926 shows Ted Anderson, the bandmaster, sitting at the front.

141 *Below left.* Members of a group of morris dancers with the cups and shields they have won. The photograph was taken *c.*1930 on the Linotype football ground. It is not known if the group was another leisure activity encouraged by the firm.

142 *Right.* The local repertory, had been formed in 1913 but their premises in a cellar of Byrom's drapery proved too small for some of their productions which were given in hired halls. The company flourished and encouraged by G.B. Shaw opened the Garrick Theatre on Barrington Road in 1932. During the Second World War the theatre was loaned to a professional company, one of whose programmes is shown here.

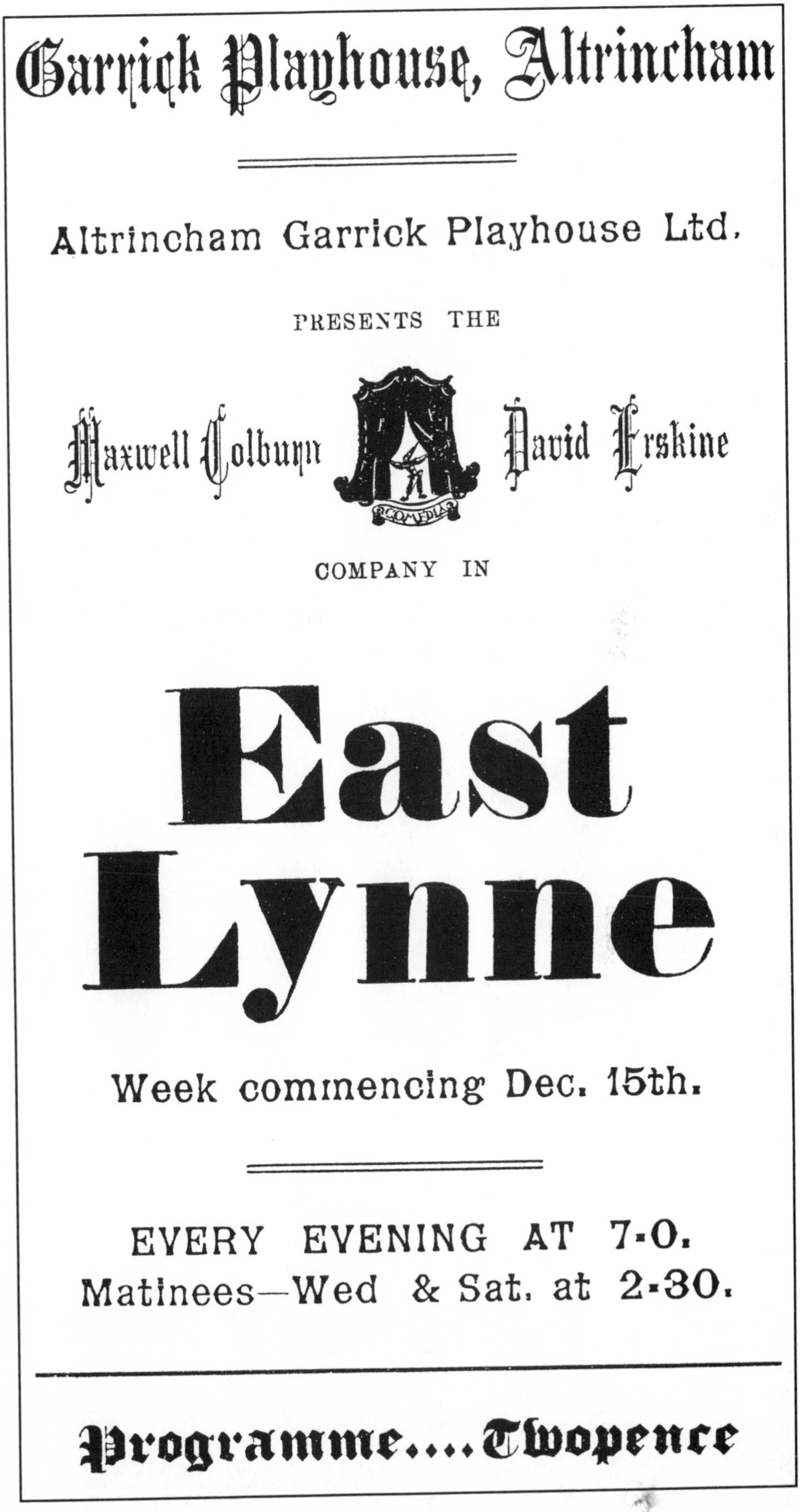

Garrick Playhouse, Altrincham

Altrincham Garrick Playhouse Ltd.

PRESENTS THE

Maxwell Colburn   David Erskine

COMPANY IN

East Lynne

Week commencing Dec. 15th.

EVERY EVENING AT 7·0.
Matinees—Wed & Sat. at 2·30.

Programme....Twopence

143 *Left*. Excavations start for the building of Schaffer Budenberg's factory, when the firm moved to Broadheath from Manchester in 1913 to manufacture gauges. The firm was expanding because of the increasing demand for instruments which would control and measure pressure accurately. Its name was changed to Budenberg Gauge Company.

144 *Below left*. The clerk of works and foreman and others oversee the pile-driving work for the hoist-well for the stairs and tower at the Budenberg's site. The tower had to have a reinforced base to compensate for the sandy nature of the ground and to support the column of mercury five storeys high which was used to calibrate the gauges.

145 *Below*. Budenberg's was an attractive building and the management is remembered by some former employees for its fairness and many kindnesses.

146 *Above*. During the First World War Budenberg's was taken over by the British Crown but continued in production. After the end of hostilities Budenberg's regained control of the factory. This picture shows the belt-driven machinery, glass fronts and piles of brass discs used in the construction of the gauges.

147 *Above right*. Since the 1930s many gauges have been calibrated by this piece of equipment using weights instead of the column of mercury. Gauges are used, for example, in hospitals to check equipment, and the firm continues in production but on a reduced scale. However, their gauges and test-equipment are still used universally.

148 & 149 *Right*. Mr. J.W. Record, the founder of Record Electrical Company (R.E.C.), and on the extreme right is his co-principal Mr. N. Naylor in 1934. Mr. Record was a gifted electrical engineer who realised the necessity of controlling and measuring the new power, electricity. He created a 'family firm' and in 1940, when 10 gold watches were presented to employees with 25 years' service, one was presented to J.R. himself.

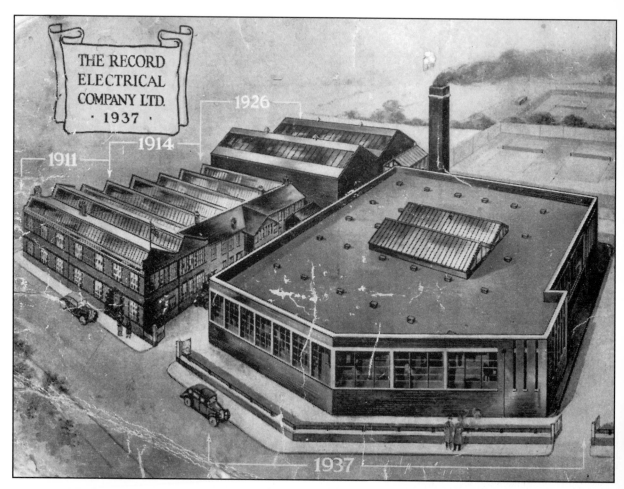

THE RECORD
ELECTRICAL
COMPANY LTD.
· 1937 ·

1911   1914   1926   1937

150 & 151 The Record Electrical Company was very successful, as its growth from 1911-37 shows. The picture of the building in 1937 shows the area surrounding the premises to be countrified whereas in fact it was completely built-up by this time. The building was refurbished in 1986 by Mr. K. Cooper and divided into small units, one of which is still occupied by R.E.C.

152 The Board Room at R.E.C., in 1934.

153 Advertisement for a tachometer, one of R.E.C.'s products. Another of their products, an A.C.-D.C. voltmeter, was calibrated on 13 January 1928 and, when tested over 60 years later, was accurate to half of one per cent.

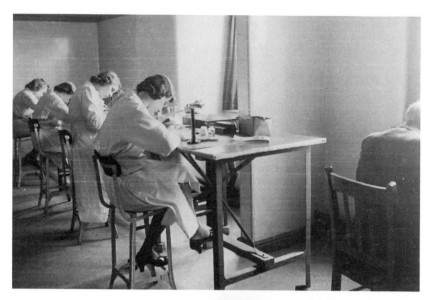

154 Luminisers at work painting the figures on the dials of some of the R.E.C. products so that the readings can be seen in the dark.

155 The employees' cycle-shed shows that cycling was a popular method of transport to work before the era of car ownership.

156 Thornton-Pickard, one of the world's major camera and shutter makers, moved to Broadheath in 1891. The photograph of workers going home by bicycle or on foot shows their flat-topped factory on the right with George Richard's engineering works behind. The workplace obviously closed down for the lunch break.

157 During the First World War Thornton-Pickard's developed a camera capable of taking aerial photographs. The photograph shows a plane with the camera mounted at the side of the cockpit, from which the camera was operated by a pull-cord. (Imperial War Museum.)

158 The Thornton-Pickard Hythe Camera Mark III was developed in 1916. Sightings of moving targets were photographed, enabling trainee-gunners to improve their expertise. The magazine for the bullets and the box for the film can be clearly seen.

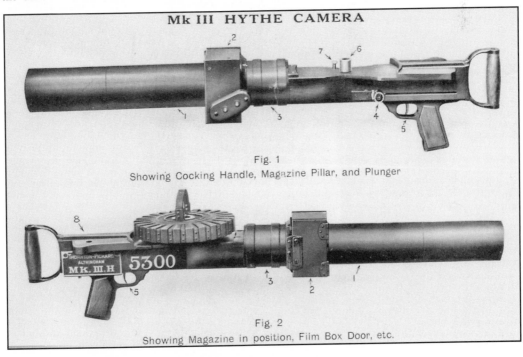

Mk III HYTHE CAMERA

Fig. 1
Showing Cocking Handle, Magazine Pillar, and Plunger

Fig. 2
Showing Magazine in position, Film Box Door, etc.

159 The photograph of this plane was taken with the Thornton-Pickard Hythe Camera Mark III. The plane was an Armstrong Whitworth FK3 (Imperial War Museum).

160 Kearns was a producer of machine-tools with a high international reputation. It commenced operations in Broadheath in 1907. Some large pieces of equipment were moved by horse-drawn lorries. This photograph shows the last load to be transported in this way.

161 One of the first pieces of Kearns equipment to be delivered by a steam-driven lorry.

162 *Above*. Gas had been part of the Altrincham scene since 1844 when the landlord of the *Unicorn*, Mr. G. Massey produced gas to light a lamp outside his inn. The Altrincham Gas Company was formed, built this complex on a field on Moss Lane and started to produce gas in 1847. Gas was sold by the cubic foot and in 1847 the cost of 1,000 cubic feet was 10s. By 1901 the cost of the same quantity was 3s.

163 *Below*. This steam-driven lorry transported bi-products from the gas works on Moss Lane. Gas was initially used to light lamps but other uses were soon realised and the industry grew. By 1919 the town was lit by 650 incandescent gas lamps.

164 *Right*. Troops of a Manchester regiment in Old Market Place in 1904. Many years earlier, in 1745, a detachment of the Pretender's Army is understood to have arrived here and demanded lodging at the *Red Lion*, then a modest inn, and other hostelries. The troop was acting as a decoy while Prince Charles and the main body of the army travelled via Stockport on their way to Derby.

165 *Above*. Some survivors and council officials gather round a memorial which was unveiled by Lord Stamford on 15 April 1919 to honour men from Chapel Street who had died in the First World War. From 66 houses, 161 men had volunteered but only 111 returned.

166 *Right*. In July 1919 a copy of this letter was presented to every child in Altrincham. It was signed by the Court Leet mayor as well as the Chairman of the Council and both their shields and mottoes appear at the top of the letter.

Altrincham
Peace Celebrations.

ARMS OF ALTRINCHAM.

JULY 17, 1919.

ARMS OF COURT LEET.

To the children of the Altrincham Schools on the day set apart for thanksgiving and rejoicing for the signing of Peace.

Dear Children,

On this ever to be remembered day when we celebrate the signing of a Great Peace at the close of the Greatest and most Terrible War in the History of the World, we call you to thanks giving, and we welcome you to the feast, and to the games and sports planned for this afternoon. May you have a full and happy day, and never forget it, or the reason why the ancient town of Altrincham invites its young people to rejoice together. We all rejoice with you because this Country has agreed, with all the other countries who have fought with it, to preserve rights and freedom to all nations; to join a great League the object of which shall be to make wars impossible. Their first step has been taken in laying a foundation upon which a lasting Peace of the World is to be built up.

We all offer to Almighty God our heartfelt thanks that he has, by the valour of our Sailors and Soldiers, under direction of great Generals, granted to us to overcome the enemy that had determined to take from us our freedom.

We do not forget those who have fallen, who will never return to the town, nor their friends who are left to mourn for them.

It should be our purpose in life to strive to make it certain that no sacrifice shall have been made in vain.

For you children in the Schools there is work to do for your Country by helping to make the town a better and brighter place to live in for old and young; just as it is for us, who are older, to work and plan to leave all ready for you to carry on when the time comes for you to take charge of its affairs. Many of you younger children have no memories of days of peace and plenty, but if we all do our part and under God's blessing, the days to come may be far happier than any that have gone before war raged with all its attendant sorrows.

Now let us enter into the full enjoyment of this happy day of Peace Celebration.

Signed on behalf of the Urban District Council and the Old Court Leet.

W. G. TAYLOR,
Chairman.

G. FAULKNER ARMITAGE,
Mayor.

167 The miniature Bavarian Castle was constructed by German and Austrian prisoners-of-war in their compound at Dunham Park. Viewing it are Mr. S. Garner, Mayor of Altrincham, Mr. S. Mayer, Mayor of Sale, Mr. B. Finch, Town Clerk of Sale and the Commanding Officer of the Camp.

168 A record of the visit to Broadheath by King George VI and Queen Elizabeth to acknowledge the part the firms there had played in the successful outcome of the Second World War.

169 Fireplace in Small Library, an interior designed by George Faulkner Armitage who lived at Stamford House, now the site of the *Cresta Court Hotel*. Mayor of Altrincham 1913-18, he was a nationally known designer and architect, producing interiors for many London clubs and country houses.

170 Sitting room interior designed by Mr. Armitage whose work was so well regarded on the continent that he won a prestigious award in Paris for one of his designs. He designed without a fee and partly presented the war memorial in the park opposite St Margaret's Church.

171 Ronald Gow was a pupil (see illustration 52) and later a teacher at the County High School. He wrote many plays and was a pioneer in the use of film-making for educational purposes. Wearing a white helmet, he directs pupils making a film of one of his own plays *The Glittering Sword*.

172 Mr. Gow encourages a young player while another of his pupils operates the camera. Some of Gow's films were shown on general release. He achieved great success with his adaptation of Walter Greenwood's story *Love on the Dole*. Leaving school-teaching, he concentrated on writing plays for the theatre and scripts for films and television. A blue plaque has been installed on the wall of the bank in Railway Street, to record where he lived as a child when his father was the manager there; another has been unveiled at the school.

OFFICERS APPOINTED AT
THE COURT LEET
OF
The Trustees of the late Right Honorable George Harry Earl of Stamford and Warrington,
HOLDEN FOR
THE BOROUGH OF ALTRINCHAM,
On Wednesday, the 24th day of October, 1883.

MAYOR.
HENRY BALSHAW, Esq., DUNHAM ROAD.

CONSTABLES.
Mr. GEORGE RICHARDSON.   Mr. THOMAS CLARKE.

DEPUTY CONSTABLE.
SUPERINTENDENT LEIGHTON.

ASSISTANT CONSTABLES.
Mr. THOMAS HANCOCK.   Mr. GEORGE HARRY WARRINGTON.

BURGESSES.
Mr. EUSTACE GEORGE PARKER.   Mr. THOMAS HANCOCK.

BYE-LAW MEN.
Mr. THOMAS HANCOCK.   Mr. GEORGE HARRY WARRINGTON.

ALE TASTERS.
Mr. JOHN LEWIS.   Mr. WILLIAM HENRY PUGH.

COMMON LOOKERS.
Mr. THOMAS WARRINGTON.   Mr. THOMAS BROCKLEHURST.

DOG MUZZLERS.
Mr. MATTHEW OKELL.   Mr. WILLIAM HENRY PUGH.

CHIMNEY LOOKER.
SERGEANT STANLEY.

MARKET LOOKERS.
Mr. THOMAS WARRINGTON.   Mr. WILLIAM TURTON.

SWINE LOOKERS.
Mr. GEORGE BOWEN.   Mr. GEORGE HARRY WARRINGTON.

BELLMAN.
Mr. ROBERT WHITHEAD.

173 This list dated 24 October 1883 gives the names of the burgesses of the Court Leet and the historic tasks to which they were appointed for that year. Some of these jobs were obsolete; others were undertaken in reality by officers of the Board of Health and other paid personnel. However the post of mayor was still a respected position which could only be held by a burgess. After the formation of the Urban District Council its head was called chairman to avoid any confusion.

174 Mr. and Mrs. Gray Pickard were Mayor and Mayoress for 1928. Mr. Pickard is wearing the mayoral red robe trimmed with black velvet and fitch (pole cat), which was presented to the town by Dr. W.A. Renshaw. This useful garment can easily be altered to fit any size of man elected to the office. The gold chain is formed of links bearing the names of many previous mayors.

175 In 1937 Altrincham was granted a Charter to become a Municipal Borough. The posts of Mayor of the Court Leet and Chairman of the Council were fused and the Earl of Stamford became the Charter Mayor. He is shown at the ceremony (left to right): Mr. W. Waterhouse, Deputy Charter Mayor, Mr. E. Webb, Chairman of the Council, Mr. A. Glossop, Town Clerk, Earl of Stamford and Sir W. Bromley-Davenport.

The Borough of
Altrincham
Charter Celebrations
July Thirty-First 1937

176 A new coat-of-arms was blazoned for the Municipal Borough which incorporated the wheat sheaves of Cheshire (representing agriculture and farming) and a gear wheel (representing the industry at Broadheath) on the shield. The supporters wear the shields of the Earl of Stamford and of Massey. The motto was 'Altrincham en avant'—Altrincham leads the way.

177 The Market Hall, built on the corner of Market Street and Shaw's Lane, was opened in 1879. The market was started by a bell being rung by the market superintendent whereupon the traders dashed to secure a stall. Extra stalls were put on adjoining land and this area was roofed with glass c.1930 to provide cover for the traders and shoppers. Receipts for the letting of market stalls in 1937 netted £4,942. In 1990 a Blue Plaque was mounted on the wall of the hall to record the purchase from Lord Stamford of the rights to hold a market originally granted to Hamon de Massey in 1290 by Edward I.

Select Bibliography

Bamford, F., *The Making of Altrincham* (1992)

Bayliss, D.G. (ed.), *Altrincham - a History* (1992)

Bayliss, D.G. (ed.), 'A Cheshire Market Town in Victorian Times - Altrincham in 1841', Occasional Paper No.5, Altrincham History Society (AHS) (1994)

Dore, R.N., *The Civil Wars in Cheshire* (1966)

Faulkner, P., *Flashback* (1988)

Hill, C., 'The Other Altrincham Gas Works', *Link-Up*, North West Gas House Magazine (1986)

Littler, J., *The Protector of Dunham Massey* (1993)

Nickson, C., *Bygone Altrincham* (1935)

Ormerod, G., *The History of the County Palatine of Chester*, 2nd edn. (1882), Vol.1

Rendell, D., *The Thornton-Pickard Story* (1992)

Richards, R., *Old Cheshire Churches* (1947)

Richbell, D., 'Victorian Stained Glass', *AHS Journal No. 2* (December, 1991)

Index

Roman numerals refer to pages in the Introduction, and arabic numerals to individual illustrations